# WASHINGTON
*on my mind*

FALCON

The ridges of Mt. Shuksan, in North Cascades National Park, blush with alpenglow in the evening light   TERRY DONNELLY

*"Out of the forest at last there stood the mountain, wholly unveiled, awful in bulk and majesty, filling all the view like a separate, newborn world, yet withal so fine and so beautiful it might well fire the dullest observer to desperate enthusiasm."*

John Muir

4

Commercial fishing boats at Seattle's Fishermen's Terminal await the opening of a new fishing season   H. RICHARD JOHNSTON

An abandoned schoolhouse near Kamiak Butte moored in an ocean of wheat   DARRELL GULIN

A perfect reflection in the tranquil waters of Naiad Lake   KEITH LAZELLE

Old-world charm graces this cottage on Vashon Island   TERRY DONNELLY

The delicate blossoms of spring in Snohomish   ANN CECIL

Time stands still at Riverfront Park in Spokane   AUDREY GIBSON

Dawn comes to Seattle's world-famous public market at the foot of Pike Street   TERRY DONNELLY

*"There was something about the exuberance of the frontier in what residents liked to call the 'Seattle spirit'. . . . [Seattle's] success was a triumph for generations of frontier optimists who had dreamed of a thriving city rising out of the wilderness to traffic in silk and gold as well as salmon and lumber. . . ."*

Earl Pomeroy,
*The Pacific Slope: A History of California,
Oregon, Washington, Idaho, Utah, and Nevada*

On New Year's Eve, the Seattle Space Needle blooms with a frond of fireworks   KEITH LAZELLE

Seattle celebrates one of its favorite sons with this mural of Jimi Hendrix  SCOTT T. SMITH

Volkswagens beware: The troll under Seattle's Fremont Street Bridge has quite an appetite   SCOTT T. SMITH

As silent as wings over water, a crew of boatmen glide through the fog   TOM & PAT LEESON

*"Every part of this soil is sacred in the estimation of my people. Every hillside, every valley, every plain and grove has been hallowed by some sad or happy event in days long vanished. Even the rocks, which seem to be dumb and dead as they swelter in the sun along the silent shore, thrill with memories. . . ."*

Chief Seattle at the signing of the
Treaty of Port Elliott, 1855

A Makah Indian girl helps bake salmon the traditional way in Neah Bay
TOM & PAT LEESON

A pictograph of "She Who Watches" enlivens a rocky hillside near the Columbia River   PAT O'HARA

Moss drapes over bigleaf maples in the Hoh Rain Forest, Olympic National Park   CHARLES GURCHE

Lush vegetation adorns the gorge of the Ohanapecosh River below Silver Falls  TERRY DONNELLY

One tree nurses on another in the Olympic National Forest  DAVE SCHIEFELBEIN

"Whenever we took the trail we stepped into a strange, soft world of silent moss. We walked as if shod with felt slippers; our knees slid through climbs of ferns. Sometimes the ferns rioted over the pile carpet and up the tree trunks. But the carpet climbed the tree trunks, too, as far as the eye could see; a green, gray, bluish yellow moss carpet—from which sword ferns and lady ferns sprayed like garlands."

Roger Tory Peterson & James Fisher,
*Wild America*

Sunset paints the tidal flats surrounding the dramatic sea stacks at Second Beach, on the Olympic Peninsula   JACK DYKINGA

"That rugged coast, a narrow seam between forest and sea. . . . Its prehistoric ramparts have been invaded by the sea, leaving ancient nearshore ruins: stubborn, surreal stone castles— sentinel sea stacks sprinkled with spruce and the nests of auklets. It is a broken sawblade of a coast, its battle with the sea one of violence and beauty."

David Hooper,
*Exploring Washington's Wild Olympic Coast*

Balsamroot, lupine, and oak trees tell their stories in the Columbia River Gorge National Scenic Area   STEVE TERRILL

A dew-drenched balsamroot is the very picture of spring   CRAIG TUTTLE

The American goldfinch is a late spring migrant   SCOTT PRICE

A tree frog hides among paintbrush leaves in an area devastated by Mount St. Helens just a few years ago   STEVE TERRILL

The many colors of nature's bounty at Pike Place Market in Seattle   TERRY DONNELLY

"*From one end to the other, [Washington] is the land of tall trees and tall men, of the apple, the peach, the prune, and the pine; the land of the green valley and the rushing river. The rosy pink of its orchards every spring is equalled only by the sunset glow upon its peaks of eternal snow. It is the charmed land of the American continent. . . . what the climate of heaven must be like.*"

Woods Hutchinson

Happiness is a big pumpkin patch   ANN CECIL

A sea of cabbages flourishes in the summer sun   TOM & PAT LEESON

Water is a major industry in Washington, as it is here at Diablo Dam, in Ross Lake National Recreation Area   DAVE SCHIEFELBEIN

*"Grand Coulee is indeed special, the largest man-made creation on this earth, four times the size of the Great Pyramid and dwarfing the tall buildings of our modern cities."*

Ellis Lucia,
*This Land Around Us: A Treasury of Pacific Northwest Writing*

The Grand Coulee Dam, called "the biggest thing built by the hand of humans," is the world's largest producer of hydroelectric power

Winter sculpts its own version of fir branches at the edge of the Mt. Baker-Snoqualmie National Forest    TERRY DONNELLY

Ice crystals enlace river rocks at the edge of the North Fork Nooksack River   TERRY DONNELLY

Mount Rainier rises into a vivid sky as dawn breaks over the Tahlequah ferry dock on Vashon Island   TERRY DONNELLY

The streets come alive in springtime in Seattle's Pioneer Square
ANN CECIL

Autumn sun gilds Roche Harbor on San Juan Island
TOM & PAT LEESON

Mount Shuksan, in the North Cascade Range, is the thirteenth tallest peak in Washington   CRAIG TUTTLE

An old barn surrenders to time in a harvested wheat field
DAVE SCHIEFELBEIN

*“[Washington] is a continental micro-
cosm, only it's been laid out backward. The
deserts, badlands, canyons, and wheat fields
of the western American landscape lie in
eastern Washington, and the bustling cities
and serene seaside settlements of a New
England lie along Washington's western
coast, with two white-capped mountain
ranges for backdrop, and rain forests of
almost Amazonian density thrown in for
good measure.”*

Andrew Ward,
*Out Here: A Newcomer's Notes from the Great Northwest*

The noble crest of Mount Rainier rises over its placid kingdom at Tipsoo Lake   H. RICHARD JOHNSTON

*“We had rounded a point, . . . when I, lifting sleepy eyelids . . . was suddenly aware of a vast white shadow in the water. What cloud, piled massive on the horizon, could cast an image so sharp in outline, so full of vigorous detail of surface? No cloud, as my stare, no longer dreamy, presently discovered—no cloud, but a cloud compeller. It was a giant mountain dome of snow, swelling and seeming to fill the aerid spheres as its image displaced the blue deeps of tranquil water.”*

Theodore Winthrop, 1853

Sam Hill, Quaker and apostle of peace, built a full-scale replica of Stonehenge in the 1920s to honor those killed in World War I
TERRY DONNELLY

A half-moon in the evening sky aspires to the fullness of a Port Townsend clock tower   TOM & PAT LEESON

A massive tree trunk emerges like the prow of a ghost ship from the gravel of Lisabeula Beach    TERRY DONNELLY

A sea arch provides a gilt-edged frame for the Olympic National Park coastline at sunset   TOM TILL

*"The Pacific is my home ocean; I knew it first, grew up on its shore, collected marine animals along the coast. I know its moods, its color, its nature. It was very far inland that I caught the first smell of the Pacific. . . . I believe I smelled the sea rocks and the kelp and the iodine and the under odor of washed and ground calcareous shells. Such a far-off and remembered odor comes subtly so that one does not consciously smell it, but rather an electric excitement is released —a kind of boisterous joy. I found myself plunging over the roads of Washington, as dedicated to the sea as any migrating lemming."*

John Steinbeck,
*Travels with Charley*

A sea star gleams in the still waters of a tidepool   JAMES O. SNEDDON

Christine Falls cascades beneath a stone bridge over Van Trump Creek   TERRY DONNELLY

A hikers' shelter nestles among evergreens on the trail to Soleduck Falls, Olympic National Park   RICK SCHAFER

Autumn leaves drop like jewels on the banks of Riley Falls,
Mount Adams Wilderness Area   CRAIG TUTTLE

Fort Vancouver mountain man Barney Swanson
recalls the life of a trapper in the 1800s
TOM & PAT LEESON

*Real rough, red-blooded, burly,
bully, savage, dirt-stomping, ear-
chewing, tobacco-loving, whisker-
growing, hell-roaring He Men. . . . "*

James Stevens,
*Paul Bunyan*

On a winter morning at Lyle Point, the simple grace of a teepee encampment  DANIEL DANCER

An old-growth forest of Douglas-fir and western hemlock, Thorton T. Munger Research Natural Area   TERRY DONNELLY

A squirrel pilfers goods from the forest floor   SCOTT PRICE

*"In passing through the forest one may wander a whole day and see no living thing save a squirrel, whose shrill chatter is startling amid the silence. The wind plays in the tree-tops far overhead, but seldom stirs the branches of the smaller growth. The great tree trunks stand immovable."*

Bailey Willis, 1881

Some of the world's largest trees inhabit Washington's forests
PAT O'HARA

Japanese cherry trees bloom along Azalea Way at the Washington Park Arboretum in Seattle   TERRY DONNELLY

Frost on a crisp winter morning at the Snoqualmie train depot  STEVE TERRILL

An abandoned mill offers mute testimony to the bustling history of the agriculturally rich Palouse region RICK SCHAFER

Wild roses cup the golden afternoon light in the meadows of Steptoe Butte State Park   KEITH LAZELLE

*"The day is real; the sky clicks securely in place over the mountains, locks round the islands, snaps slap on the bay. Air fits flush on farm roofs; it rises inside the doors of barns and rubs at yellow barn windows. Air clicks up my hand cloven into fingers and wells in my ears' holes, whole and entire. I call it simplicity, the way matter is smooth and alone."*

Annie Dillard,
*Holy the Firm*

Two friends enjoy a summer evening in Whitman County   SCOTT PRICE

An old barn near Cinebar stands guard in a field of wildflowers   SCOTT T. SMITH

The peaks of the Tatoosh Range rise above the fog at first light   H. RICHARD JOHNSTON

*"... the inhabitants of that area led a literally sheltered life ... enclosed between the Cascades just to the east and the Olympic Range across the Sound to the west. Even when fog, rain, or snow made the mountains invisible, we felt their mitigating presence.... It was like living in the hollow of the cupped hand of God."*

Richard L. Williams,
*The Cascades*

Biplanes and retired military aircraft still fly at Seattle's Museum of Flight   CRAIG TUTTLE

The Boeing Aircraft Company supplies jets to airlines worldwide and is Washington's largest employer   TOM & PAT LEESON

Washington's capitol dome gleams on a bright Olympia day   PAT O'HARA

The Paradise River washes over rocky falls in early autumn   TERRY DONNELLY

*"In the beginning of the world, all was water."*

Yakama Indian origin story

A steelhead jumps a waterfall   TOM & PAT LEESON

Salmon makes a sporting lunch for one happy black bear   TOM & PAT LEESON

In late summer, an exuberance of pink geraniums welcomes visitors to the Volunteer Park Conservatory and gardens TERRY DONNELLY

A male mountain bluebird graces a tree branch in the Colville National Forest   SCOTT PRICE

A dragon in Seattle's International District looms over a girl feeding pigeons   H. RICHARD JOHNSTON

Cherry blossoms festoon a Japanese lantern in the Kobe Terrace above Seattle's International District   TERRY DONNELLY

A kayaker takes some spray during the White Salmon River kayakers' competition   CHARLIE BORLAND/BORLAND STOCK PHOTO

*"One who runs these rivers has the sense of being primitive man pitted against the elements. His skills, his endurance are all that count. There is no community to underwrite his errors, to make up for his mistakes. All that matters is his skill, and his alone."*

William O. Douglas,
*My Wilderness: The Pacific West*

Rafters get a happy soaking on the Wenatchee River
TOM & PAT LEESON

A windsurfer on the Columbia River catches some air   MIKE BELOZER/BORLAND STOCK PHOTO

An old wooden fishing boat gets refurbished at Port Townsend  TOM & PAT LEESON

Water-wizened seine net floats are ready for the next fishing season
CURT GIVEN

Old queens of the harbor are a common yet evocative sight at Fishermen's Terminal in Seattle   TERRY DONNELLY

A sailor adjusts the rigging on Puget Sound   SCOTT T. SMITH

Two old fishing friends on a beach in Olympic National Park wait for their morning catch    PAT O'HARA

A water baby tickling his toes in the wavelets of Puget Sound
SCOTT T. SMITH

*"Nothing can be more striking than the beauty of these waters without a shoal or a rock or any danger whatever for the whole length of this internal navigation, the finest in the world. Nothing can exceed the beauty of these waters and their safety. I venture nothing in saying that there is no country in the world that possesses waters equal to these."*

Captain George Vancouver describing Puget Sound

“*I like to put my pack under a spruce and lie in the grass above the beach, watching the waves come in from Asia. When the wind is high there is always a booming sound from the nearby point. When the air is breathless, the waves are soft and gentle and faraway. Then the quiet of the bench above the beach is so quiet I have heard the pods of the brome grass breaking. . . . I realize how small and minute man is in the cosmic scheme.*”

William O. Douglas,
*My Wilderness: The Pacific West*

North Head Light stands guard over the Washington coastline  H. RICHARD JOHNSTON

A shipload of Sitka spruce logs is loaded aboard the *Tokai Maru* for its trans-Pacific voyage   CURT GIVEN

Sorting through a mountain of logs at Longview   CHARLIE BORLAND/BORLAND STOCK PHOTO

A logger near Vader hoists his chainsaw after a hard day's work
CHARLIE BORLAND/BORLAND STOCK PHOTO

*"Oh! What timber. . . . Forests in which you cannot ride a horse—in which you cannot possibly recover game you have shot without the help of a good retriever—forests into which you cannot see, and which are almost dark under a midday sun—such forests, containing firs, cedars, pine, spruce, and hemlock, envelop Puget Sound and cover a large part of Washington Territory, surpassing the woods of all the rest of the globe in the size, quantity, and quality of the timber."*

Samuel Wilkerson, 1869

The Forks Timber Museum celebrates the history of logging on the Olympic Peninsula   JAMES RANDKLEV

Iron wagon wheels fence in an old barn and silo near Uniontown, eastern Washington   DARRELL GULIN

A boatload of colorful mailboxes serves the houseboat community on Seattle's Lake Union
TERRY DONNELLY

*66*Only a few ranchers and assorted iconoclasts live here. When I asked one of them why people homesteaded this tough land, he grinned at me. 'Some people came here,' he said, '*because* it couldn't be plowed.' *99*

Michael Parfit,
"The Floods That Carved the West," *Smithsonian*

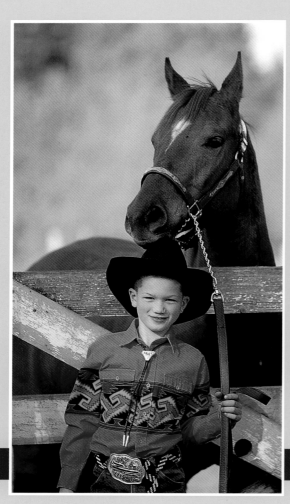

A young cowboy and friend look forward to a good day of riding in Marysville ANN CECIL

Antlers, artifacts, and Old Glory decorate a redwood barn in Yakima   H. RICHARD JOHNSTON

A mountain biker enjoys a high alpine trail   KIRKENDALL & SPRING/BORLAND STOCK PHOTO

Fighting stiff competition in the National Bike Race at Alki Point   DARRELL GULIN

The wheat fields of the Palouse area in eastern Washington are among the most productive in the nation   CHARLES GURCHE

A lustrous trio of hot-air balloons ascends during Walla Walla's annual Balloon Stampede   DEBI OTTINGER

Afternoon sun rakes the rippled fields of the Palouse region   CRAIG TUTTLE

A tractor ready for work in the fertile barley and wheat fields of the Palouse   CRAIG TUTTLE

*"The hills roll on and on. Treeless, their gentle contours seem sculpted, as if they were formed not by natural forces but an unusually conscientious pastry chef. This is the Palouse, a region unlike any other, where the plow knows every acre but no furrow runs straight."*

Fred Brack and Tina Bell,
*Tastes of the Pacific Northwest*

A field of wildflowers graces the foothills of Mount Baker CHARLES GURCHE

This Queen Anne-style mansion at Fort Vancouver was once the home of George C. Marshall   TERRY DONNELLY

*"Here in the corner attic of America, two hours' drive from a rain forest, a desert, a foreign country, an empty island, a hidden fjord, a raging river, a glacier, and a volcano is a place where the inhabitants sense they can do no better, nor do they want to."*

Timothy Egan,
*The Good Rain: Across Time and Terrain in the Pacific Northwest*

A Snohomish five-year-old gets a kiss from a friend
ANN CECIL

A Bohemian waxwing perches among mountain ash berries   DONALD M. JONES

Fall paints a vine maple exotic colors in the North Fork Nooksack River Valley   TERRY DONNELLY

A farmstead surrounded by a field of tulips in Skagit County  CHARLES GURCHE

The tulip fields of the Skagit Valley enchant thousands of visitors every year   ANN CECIL

A Mount Vernon painter captures the transitory beauty of springtime   ANN CECIL

87

Two weathered open boats at the Center for Wooden Boats on Lake Union   TERRY DONNELLY

*"When the fog cleared off . . . we enjoyed the delightful prospect of the ocean; that ocean, the object of all our labors, the reward of all our anxieties."*

Meriwether Lewis

Retiring the colors at Roche Harbor on San Juan Island   RICK SCHAFER

Three Elliott Bay kayakers watch the sun set over the Olympic Mountains   RICK SCHAFER

A blacksmith in period dress works at the forge in Fort Vancouver   TOM & PAT LEESON

Cobbler Dave Page resoles a workman's boot   CLIFF LEIGHT

A young expert shears a sheep in Clark County   TOM & PAT LEESON

*"Seattle had ships at the ends of its streets and gulls in its traffic. Its light was restless and watery, making the buildings shiver like reflections. It felt like an island and smelled of the sea."*

Jonathan Raban,
*Hunting Mister Heartbreak*

The Seattle skyline gleams at eventide from a Harbor Island pier   TERRY DONNELLY

Balsamroot, lupine, and paintbrush bring color to the verdant fields of Washington   CHARLES GURCHE

Bluebird hydrangea blossom in the Washington Park Arboretum in Seattle   TERRY DONNELLY

Lupine and tiger lilies are among the wildflowers found in the Columbia River Gorge   H. RICHARD JOHNSTON

A mule deer fawn nuzzles its mother   DARRELL GULIN

A tiny, elusive pika in the rock slides of Rainier National Park
CURT GIVEN

Sandstone formations provide an eerie foreground to Manastash Ridge  CHARLES GURCHE

This photo of Mount St. Helens was taken a month after it erupted in May 1980  RUSSELL D. LAMB

Mount St. Helens in quiet repose   CRAIG TUTTLE

*"On May 17, 1980, Mount St. Helens was a symmetrical cone, a mountain so near perfection it was sometimes called 'America's Mount Fujiyama.' Photographers loved St. Helens because it looked the way a mountain is supposed to look: smooth sides, pointed crest, fluted topping of snow. . . . It was a scene made for calendars and postcards. That was May 17. By the evening of May 18, Mount St. Helens was a smoking crater, hollowed-out and grey."*

Rob Carson,
*Mount St. Helens: The Eruption and Recovery of a Volcano*

Ash plumes catch the setting sun the day
Mount St. Helens erupted   TOM & PAT LEESON

The Olympic National Forest shoulders a mantle of fog   CRAIG TUTTLE

Residents of Maury Island rely on boats of all kinds for their transportation TERRY DONNELLY

> **"**Fog is another matter. Fog on the beach, the foghorns speaking the language of ghost ships. Fog in the forest, turning the trees to Japanese etchings. Fog in a meadow, a droplet sparkling on every lupine leaf. Fog around a campfire, giving you a shadow as huge as the Specter of the Brocken. Fog cools your brow and bathes your eyes and washes your whiskers and cleans the wax out of your ears. **"**
>
> Harvey Manning,
> *Washington Wilderness: The Unfinished Work*

Asters grow wild in the meadows of Mount Rainier National Park
LAURENCE PARENT

A climber on Mount Redoubt gains spectacular views of the North Cascade Range   CLIFF LEIGHT

*"The high points on the map are called
Terror, Fury, Despair, Forgotten, Forbidden,
Formidable, Freezeout, Inspiration, Triumph,
Challenger, Desolation, Isolation, Damnation,
Illusion, Joker, Nodoubt, Redoubt, Three Fools.
These are not the kind of names that come
from dull-witted surveyors or Forest Service
committees. These are climber's names."*

Timothy Egan, *The Good Rain:
Across Time and Terrain in the Pacific Northwest*

Rock climbers belay on Chianti Spire among some of Washington's
more rugged peaks   CLIFF LEIGHT

Snow crews work to open the North Cascades highway beneath the towering Liberty Bell Mountain  CLIFF LEIGHT

Fishermen cast in the placid waters of the Snoqualmie River   DARRELL GULIN

"*The people of [Washington] are seen as healthy, independent, innovative— measuring achievement as much in terms of climbing mountains as in climbing corporate ladders. Surrounded by the power and majesty of the natural world, familiar with the woods, waterways, and the high country, we are finding our identity within nature as well as within human history.*"

Nicholas O'Connell,
*At the Field's End*

A quiet moment by La Poel Creek in Olympic National Park   PAT O'HARA

Fall decorates the banks of Icicle Creek in the Wenatchee National Forest   TERRY DONNELLY

Six water lilies float in a still eddy along the Columbia River Gorge   H. RICHARD JOHNSTON

Sunset paints a golden mantle on the shoreline of Larrabee State Park   CLIFF LEIGHT

Sea otters are a favorite sight along Washington's coastline   KEN ARCHER

Traditional Northwest Coast art decorates a modern kayak and shed
CLIFF LEIGHT

Two killer whales cavort in the waters of the Strait of Juan de Fuca   JEFF FOOTT

A pod of orcas cruises off Washington's north coast   JEFF FOOTT

*"Few things set the human heart to racing as hard as the sight of black dorsal fins on the horizon. When they break the surface . . . the killers show the grace of ballerinas. . . . Through their blowholes they spout a blast as grand as a geyser gush. . . . Cleanly black-and-white, the orca would be ruined by colorization."*

Timothy Egan,
*The Good Rain: Across Time and Terrain in the Pacific Northwest*

A ring-necked pheasant cock performs his spring mating dance   TOM & PAT LEESON

*“This is undulating country, and the wheat, planted along the hills in eccentric rings and ovals, climbs up one slope and down another . . . as if somebody were running a gentle invisible thumb over orange plush.”*

John Gunther,
*Inside U.S.A.*

Trees nestle among the rolling wheat fields of Columbia County   LAURENCE PARENT

View from a barn window  DARRELL GULIN

Tillinghast Seed Co. in La Conner displays the bounties of autumn   ANN CECIL

Large bracket fungi decorate a log in the Hoh Rain Forest   JAMES RANDKLEV

*"This valley is . . . dense rain forest, and the color that predominates is green— from the thick forest canopy to the fern-draped floor. Yet the forest is no dull monotone. A hundred shades of green abound: sun-drenched treetops, blackish-green trunks strewn with chartreuse mosses, emerald ferns and shamrocklike oxalis. Eerie, leaf-filtered green light flows everywhere. . . . A damp earthy smell fills the air, and the silence seems all-encompassing."*

Tom Melham,
*John Muir's Wild America*

A rough-skinned newt relaxes on a branch   DAVE SCHIEFELBEIN

The cataract of Soleduck Falls is well worth the hike to get there   STEVE TERRILL

# *they made it possible*

*Washington on My Mind* would have been impossible to produce without the keen eyes and technical skills of more than thirty-five professional photographers. These women and men submitted their finest images, and the results show in this stunning collection of photos. What does not show is the work it took to get these images—the early mornings to capture the sunrise, the long climbs through rugged terrain, the endless hours of waiting for the perfect light, the hundreds of shots that didn't turn out quite right, and the high level of technical skills that were acquired through years of experience and study. To all the photographers who contributed to *Washington on My Mind*, we say thanks. We appreciate their art and their hard work.

Michael S. Sample and Bill Schneider
Publishers, Falcon Press

## PHOTOGRAPHERS IN *WASHINGTON ON MY MIND*

Ken Archer
Mike Belozer/
  Borland Stock Photo
Charlie Borland/
  Borland Stock Photo
Ann Cecil
Daniel Dancer
Terry Donnelly
Jack Dykinga
Jeff Foott
Audrey Gibson
Curt Given
Darrell Gulin
Charles Gurche
H. Richard Johnston
Donald M. Jones
Kirkendall & Spring/
  Borland Stock Photo

Russell B. Lamb
Keith Lazelle
Tom & Pat Leeson
Cliff Leight
Pat O'Hara
Laurence Parent
Debi Ottinger
Scott Price
James Randklev
Dave Schiefelbein
Rick Schafer
Scott T. Smith
James O. Sneddon
Steve Terrill
Tom Till
Craig Tuttle

© 1996 by Falcon Press Publishing Co., Inc.
Helena and Billings, Montana

All rights reserved, including the right to reproduce any part of this book in any form, except brief quotations for reviews, without the written permission of the publisher.

Design, typesetting, and other prepress work by Falcon Press, Helena, Montana. Printed in Korea.

Library of Congress Number: 96-85303

ISBN 1-56044-495-9

For extra copies of this book please check with your local bookstore, or write to Falcon Press, P.O. Box 1718, Helena, MT  59624 or call toll-free 1-800-582-2665.

End papers: Frosted hawthorn leaves   CHARLIE GURCHE
Title page: Mukilteo Lighthouse at sunset   TERRY DONNELLY

# *acknowledgments*

*The publisher gratefully acknowledges the following sources:*

Page 3 quoted in *John Muir's Wild America*, by Tom Melham. © 1976 by National Geographic Society, Washington, D.C.

Page 10 from *The Pacific Slope: A History of California, Oregon, Washington, Idaho, Utah, and Nevada* by Earl Pomeroy. © 1965 by Earl Pomeroy; Alfred A. Knopf, New York.

Page 14 quoted in *Seattle: The Life and Times of an American City* by Gerald B. Nelson. © 1977 by Gerald B. Nelson; Alfred A. Knopf, New York.

Page 17 from *Wild America*, by Roger Tory Peterson and James Fisher. © 1955 by Roger Tory Peterson and James Fisher; Houghton Mifflin, Boston.

Page 19 from *Exploring Washington's Wild Olympic Coast* by David Hooper. © 1993 by David Hooper; The Mountaineers, Seattle.

Page 22 quoted in "The Dawn of Tomorrow," by Robert Whitaker, in *These United States: A Symposium*, edited by Ernest Gruening. © 1924 by Boni Liveright, New York.

Page 24 from *This Land Around Us: A Treasury of Pacific Northwest Writing*, edited and with commentary by Ellis Lucia. © 1969 by Ellis Lucia; Doubleday & Company, Garden City, New York.

Page 29 from *Out Here: A Newcomer's Notes from the Great Northwest*, by Andrew Ward. © 1991 by Andrew Ward; Penguin Books, New York.

Page 31 quoted in *Mount Rainier: A Record of Exploration*, edited by Edmond S. Meany. © 1916 by Macmillan, New York.

Page 35 from *Travels with Charley*, by John Steinbeck. © 1962 by John Steinbeck; The Curtis Publishing Company, New York.

Page 38 from *Paul Bunyan*, by James Stevens. © 1925, 1947 by Alfred A. Knopf, New York, and renewed in 1953 by James Stevens.

Page 41 quoted in *Mount Rainier: A Record of Exploration*, edited by Edmond S. Meany. © 1916 by Macmillan, New York.

Page 46 from *Holy the Firm*, by Annie Dillard. © 1977 by Annie Dillard; Harper & Row, New York.

Page 49 from *The Cascades* by Richard L. Williams. © 1974 by Time-Life Books, Alexandria, Virginia.

Page 54 from *Indian Legends of the Pacific Northwest*, by Ella Clark. © 1953 by Ella Clark; University of California Press, Berkeley.

Pages 60, 66 from *My Wilderness: The Pacific West*, by William O. Douglas. © 1960 by William O. Douglas; Doubleday, New York.

Page 65 quoted in Volume II of *Northwest Passages*, by Bruce Calhoun. © 1972 by Miller Freeman Publications, Inc., San Francisco.

Page 69 quoted in *The Loggers,* Old West Series, Time-Life Books. © 1976 by Time-Life Books, Alexandria, Virginia.

Page 72 from "The Floods That Carved the West," by Michael Parfit. Published in *Smithsonian*, April 1995.

Page 79 from *Tastes of the Pacific Northwest* by Fred Brack and Tina Bell. © 1988 by Fred Brack and Tina Bell; Doubleday, New York.

Pages 83, 102, 111 from *The Good Rain: Across Time and Terrain in the Pacific Northwest*, by Timothy Egan. © 1990 by Timothy Egan; Alfred A. Knopf, New York.

Page 88 quoted in *Seattle: The Life and Times of an American City*, by Gerald B. Nelson. © 1977 by Gerald B. Nelson; Alfred A. Knopf, New York.

Page 92 from *Hunting Mister Heartbreak*, by Jonathan Raban. © 1991 by Jonathan Raban; HarperCollins Publishers, Inc., New York.

Page 99 from *Mount St. Helens: The Eruption and Recovery of a Volcano*, by Rob Carson. © 1990 by The Morning News Tribune, Tacoma; Sasquatch Books, Seattle.

Page 101 from *Washington Wilderness: The Unfinished Work*, by Harvey Manning. © 1984 by Harvey Manning, Pat O'Hara, and Richard Rutz; The Mountaineers, Seattle.

Page 104 from *At the Field's End*, by Nicholas O'Connell. © 1987 by Nicholas O'Connell; Madrona Publishers, 1987.

Page 112 from *Inside U.S.A.*, by John Gunther. © 1947 by the Curtis Publishing Company, New York.

Page 116 from *John Muir's Wild America*, by Tom Melham. © 1976 by National Geographic Society, Washington, D.C.

Page 120 from *The Alpine Lakes*, by Brock Evans. © 1971 by The Mountaineers, Seattle.

Laughingwater Creek Bridge welcomes all wanderers
PAT O'HARA

*"The long ridges, the rounded summits, of this province . . . are a land of exquisite beauty—of woodland trails with the wind sighing in the trees, of delightful little glens, of moss-banked brooks, of quiet streams. . . ."*

Brock Evans,
*The Alpine Lakes*